HORSES
and HORSEMANSHIP in the ATHENIAN AGORA

JOHN McK. CAMP II

Color Photographs by
CRAIG A. MAUZY

American School of Classical Studies at Athens

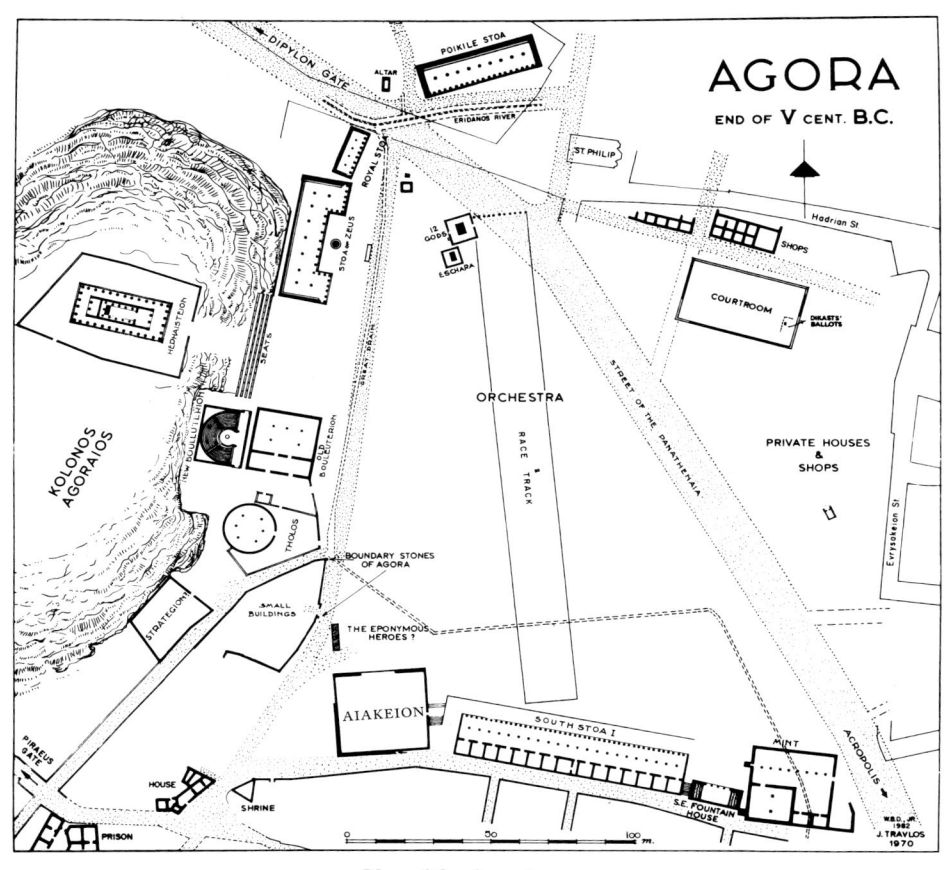

1. Plan of the Agora in ca. 400 B.C.

Horses were an integral part of life in ancient Greece; they played an active role in warfare, in transportation, and in the games which were such an important and regular feature of Greek society. Athenian enthusiasm for the horse is expressed in numerous ways in the Agora (1). Here the Athenian cavalry trained, not far from the *hipparcheion*, headquarters of its commanding officers. Here, too, some of the popular equestrian events of the Panathenaic games were held, and the Panathenaic procession, with its huge contingent of cavalry riders (28, 39), passed through on its way up to the Acropolis. Many civic buildings and temples were adorned with paintings and sculptures of riders and battle scenes showing cavalry. Honorary statues of generals or statesmen on horseback and monuments commemorating victories in the equestrian events of the games were set up in the Agora, and vases and small objects decorated with pictures of horses were sold in the marketplace in all periods. As with many other aspects of Athenian life, the Agora is an excellent place to develop and illustrate a picture of horses and horsemanship in antiquity.

MYTH *and* PREHISTORY

The horse is a relative latecomer to Greece, probably introduced at the start of the Middle Bronze Age, around 2000 B.C. The first impression made by mounted riders must have been a vivid one, perhaps giving rise to the legend of centaurs. These creatures—half man, half horse—figure prominently in both Greek mythology and art (2, 27). Theseus, the national hero of Athens, participated in a major battle between Greeks and centaurs that became a favorite theme for Athenian artists in both vase painting and sculpture. Theseus was also successful in repelling the Amazons, fierce warrior women who usually fought from horseback (3, 4). They are thought to have come from the steppes north of the Black Sea, where it is now believed the horse was first domesticated, in the years around 4000 B.C. Like the centaurs, the Amazons were a recurring and popular subject in Greek art throughout the Archaic and Classical periods.

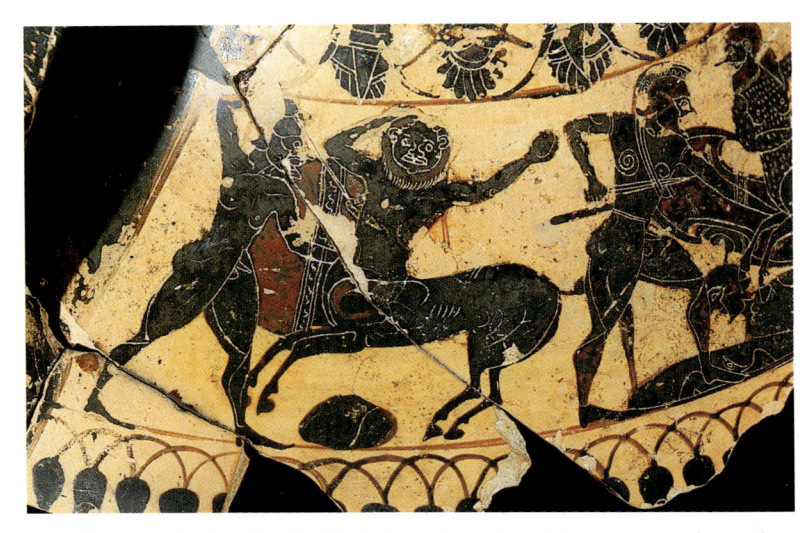

2. Centaurs fighting Greeks. Black-figured amphora, 6th century B.C. (P 13126)

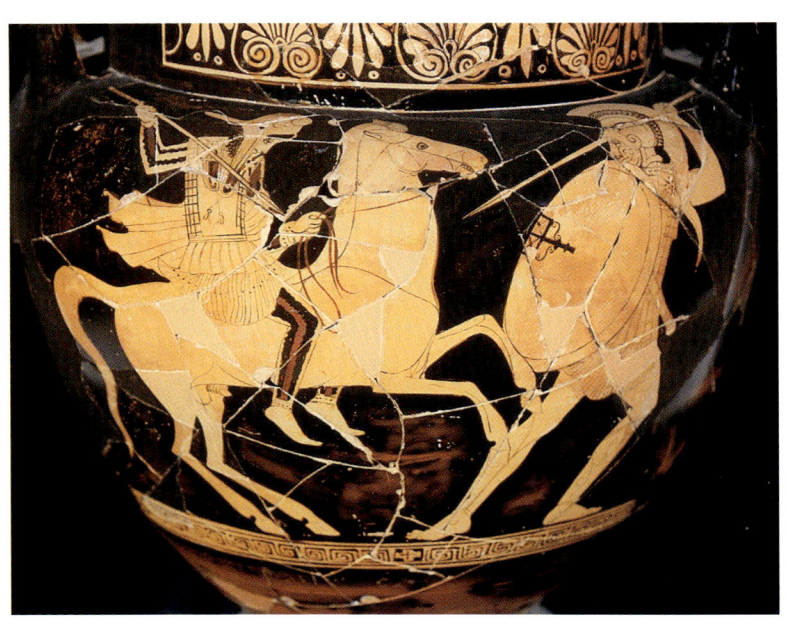

3. Mounted Amazon fighting a Greek. Red-figured krater (mixing bowl), ca. 450 B.C. (P 30197)

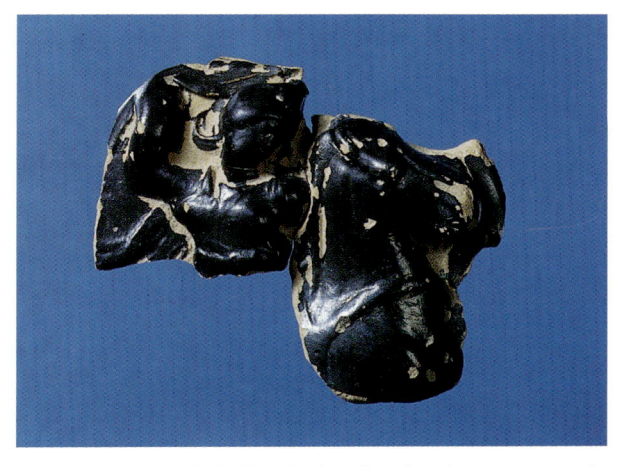

4. Fragment of a black-glazed askos, showing the upper part of a mounted Amazon. Early 4th century B.C. (P 13103)

5. Pegasos on a silver coin (drachma) of Corinth, found in the Agora. Ca. 4th century B.C. (J. H. Kroll, Agora XXVI, *no. 667)*

Other mythical beasts also had equine affinities. Most famous, of course, was the winged horse Pegasos (5, 6, 7), which came from Corinth but was popular among Athenian artists as well. Another flying equine was the *hippalektryon*, a cross between a horse and a rooster (8).

Two deities with a special interest in Athens, Athena (9, 10, 11) and her uncle Poseidon (12), together served as protectors of horses and

6. *Pegasos. Detail from a moldmade bowl, ca. 200 B.C. (P 1495) (H. Besi)*

patrons of horsemanship and equestrian activities. As such, they shared a cult on Kolonos Hippios (Horse Hill), which lay outside the city walls, not far from the Academy. Here was to be found an altar of Poseidon Hippios and Athena Hippia. The patron god of horses and earthquakes, Poseidon was the brother of Zeus and god of the sea. He was worshiped in this latter guise at the southernmost tip of Attica, at Cape Sounion, where he had a handsome marble temple in the Doric order. In Athens itself, he shared a temple on the Acropolis with Athena, and he was depicted on the west pediment of the Parthenon. According to some traditions he was also the father of Theseus. His equine interests are the subject of a chorus in Aristophanes' play *The Knights* (lines 551–560):

7. Pegasos on a black-figured amphora, 6th century B.C. (P 13027)

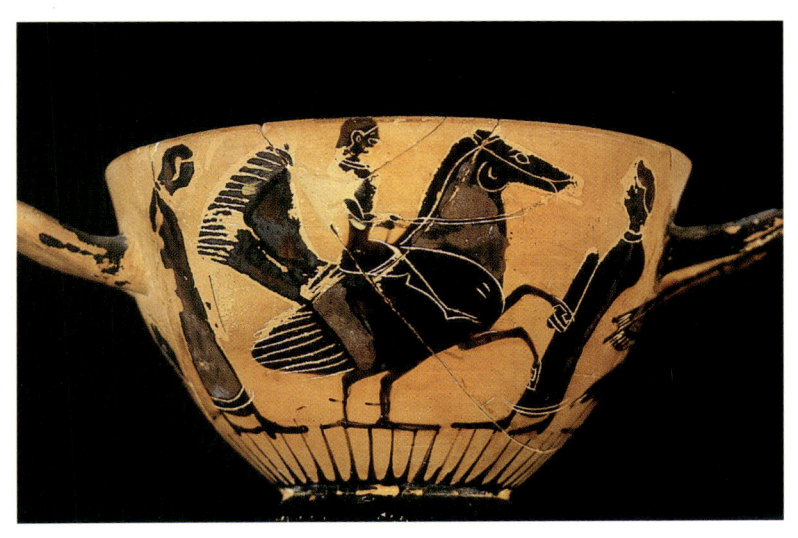

8. Hippalektryon *(horse-rooster)* on a black-figured cup, 6th century B.C. *This beast, which has no mythological story associated with it, first appears in a lost play of Aeschylus as the ensign on a ship and may have been sacred to Poseidon. About eighty-five representations are known on pots, on bronze vessels, and in sculpture.* (P 1000)

9, 10. *Athena driving a four-horse chariot* (quadriga). *Red-figured oinochoe (wine pitcher or jug), 5th century* B.C. *(P 15842)*

*11. Athena in a three-horse chariot (*triga*). Athenian bronze coin, 3rd century A.C. (AA-1030)*

12. Poseidon with his trident. Bronze coin of Demetrios Poliorcetes found in the Agora. Early 3rd century B.C. (ΙΓ 187)

Dread Poseidon, the horseman's king, you who love the brazen clash and neighing of warlike steeds. Pleased to watch where the purple-beaked trireme sweeps to the oars' long swing ... but especially where bright youths racing in their chariots flash by.

Athena, patron goddess of all Athens, was credited with the invention of the bridle and the use of chariots:

She also revealed racing chariots and war-horses and in this land first of all men the foster-child of the goddess [Erichthonios] yoked a fully equipped chariot with the aid of the goddess and revealed to all the complete art of horsemanship. (Aristeides, *Panathenaikos* 43)

Remains of actual horses have been found in a rich tholos tomb of the Late Bronze Age in Attica, at Marathon; here two animals were carefully buried facing each other in the entrance passageway (*dromos*) in the years around 1400 B.C.

13. Watercolor of a scene from the Trojan War on a Geometric oinochoe, showing war chariots. 8th century B.C. (P 4885) (P. de Jong)

The Homeric epics, which reflect this heroic age, especially the *Iliad*, are full of horses and horsemanship (13). Horses are used to draw the war chariots which deliver the heroes to the battlefield, and there are several descriptive passages of harnessing and yoking. The horses are praised for their speed and figure prominently also in a chariot race in the funeral games of Patroklos in Book 23.

HORSES and SOCIAL STATUS

Since earliest times all over the Mediterranean, the horse has been a symbol of prestige, wealth, and status. Social rank has often been defined in terms of one's ability to own and maintain a horse: the ἱππεῖς (*hippeis*) in Greece, the *equites* in Rome, or the *chevaliers* of Medieval Europe. Our own word in English, "knights," carries the same meaning.

In the Agora the earliest evidence for the association of horsemanship and high social status is found in the burials of the Iron Age cemetery which underlies the later civic center. The first is a tomb of the 9th century B.C., with rich grave goods in the form of pottery and an iron sword—in a period when such metal was still rare (14). The burial was a cremation, and found among the ashes of the pyre and the urn for the bones were two iron snaffle bits from the bridle of a horse (15). In the 8th century B.C. many of the graves contained elaborately painted cosmetic boxes (pyxides) bearing lids with handles in the form of one to four horses (16). In Athenian society of the early 6th century B.C., the second-highest property classification was a group known as the knights (*hippeis*). Thus it now seems clear from the grave goods in these early burials that our recognition of the horse as a token of high social and political status should be pushed back several centuries, to the 9th or 8th century B.C.

Throughout the 6th century B.C. Athens was ruled by several large aristocratic families who took pride in their nobility. One expression of that pride was the association of one's name with horses, and several prominent Athenians had names starting or ending with the word *hippos* (17, 18). Perhaps the earliest example is Hippothoon, one of the

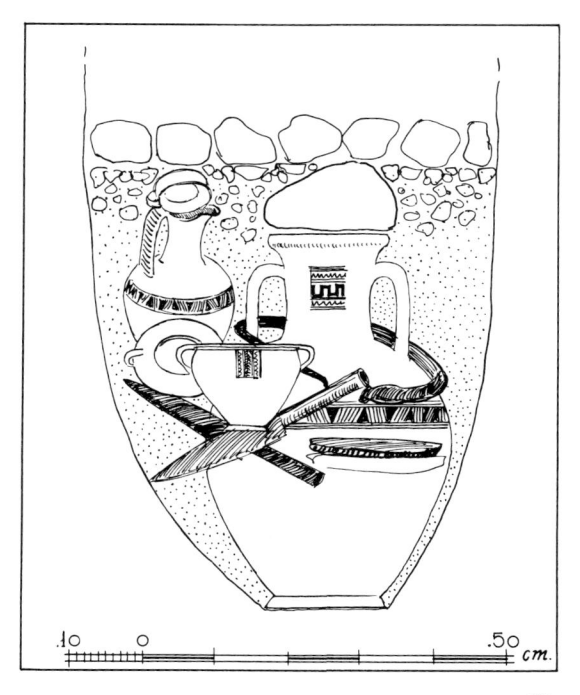

14. Cremation burial with bridle bits of iron (not shown) and an iron sword wrapped around the urn. 9th century B.C. (J. Travlos)

15. Snaffle-type bridle bits of iron from a cremation burial (14). 9th century B.C. (IL 1063, 1064)

ten eponymous heroes of Athens and the son of Poseidon. The two sons of the tyrant Peisistratos were named Hippias and Hipparchos, and the father of Perikles himself bore the name Xanthippos (18).

These old aristocratic families do not disappear with the advent of democracy at the end of the 6th century, and the association with horses in Athenian nomenclature continues well into the Classical period. There are literally hundreds of late examples of equine names. In his play *The Clouds* (423 B.C.), Aristophanes clearly and specifically

16. Pyxis (cosmetic container) with a horse handle, 8th century B.C. (P 5060)

addresses the deliberate use of some form of the word for horse in a personal name as an indicator of aristocratic pretensions and breeding. He paints thereby a telling picture of the tensions between aristocrat and commoner in democratic Athens. Strepsiades opens the play with a discussion of his marriage and the birth of his son, Pheidippides:

> Curses on the go-between who made me marry your mother! I lived so happily in the country, a commonplace, everyday life, but a good and easy one—had not a trouble, not a care, was rich in bees, in sheep, and in olives. Then indeed I had to marry the niece of Megakles, the son of Megakles; I belonged to the country, she was from the town; she was a haughty, extravagant woman, a true Coesyra. On the nuptial day, when I lay beside her, I was reeking with the dregs of the wine-cup, of cheese, and of wool; she was redolent with essences, saffron, voluptuous kisses, the love of spending, of good cheer and wanton delights. . . . Later,

when we had this boy, what was to be his name? It was the cause of much quarreling with my loving wife. She insisted on having some reference to a horse in his name, that he should be called Xanthippos, Charippos, or Kallippides. I wanted to name him Philonides after his grandfather. We disputed long and finally agreed on Pheidippides [thrifty + horse]. . . . She used to fondle and coax him, saying, "Oh, what a joy it will be to me when you have grown up, to see you in your chariot driving your steeds toward the town." And I would say to him, "When like your father, you will go, dressed in a skin, to fetch back your goats from Phelleus." Alas! He never listened to me and his madness for horses has shattered my fortune.

This same class distinction, actually defined by horses, is found in a speech of Lysias (24.11). The defendant, claiming a cripple's pension, must show that his use of a borrowed horse is necessary and not an expression of wealth or a claim to prestige:

But the strongest proof, gentlemen, of the fact that I mount horses because of my misfortune and not from insolence, as this man alleges, is this: if I were a man of means, I should ride on a saddled mule, and would not mount other men's horses. But in fact, as I am unable to acquire anything of the sort, I am compelled, now and again, to use other men's horses.

17. Ostrakon bearing an Athenian name with the hippos *(horse) stem: "Hippokrates, son of Alkmeonides." Ostraka were used as ballots cast to exile prominent Athenians, often aristocrats, especially in the 480s B.C. (P 6036)*

18. Ostrakon with the name "Perikles, son of Xanthippos." Mid 5th century B.C. (P 16755)

HORSES in ART

In the Bronze Age, horses were occasionally shown in chariot scenes on frescoes which adorned the walls of the great palaces, and they appear also drawing the hunting chariots on the funerary stelai set up over the rich grave circles at Mycenae. From Athens, however, we have few surviving works of art depicting horses; the representational scenes on Late Bronze Age pottery, strongly influenced by Minoan Crete, are largely restricted to octopods and other forms of marine life.

After the Dark Ages, which followed the collapse of the Mycenaean world, the horse makes its appearance among the earliest attempts at representation by Greek vase painters, in the 9th and 8th centuries B.C. The horse appears first, followed by human figures and birds, in the earliest examples of pictorial art after several centuries in which the decoration on pottery was confined to purely geometric ornament. At first the figures are simple, the forms still made up of geometric shapes done in dark silhouette against a light background (19, 20, 13). In the 7th century, larger and more realistic representations of horses appear on Protoattic vases (21, 22), and become very common on the black-figured and red-figured vases of the 6th and 5th centuries (23–25, 9, 10, 37, 38).

Though they do not survive today, monumental paintings adorned the walls of many public buildings in the Agora, and they often depicted cavalry battles. One of Aristophanes' characters (*Lysistrata* 677–679) refers to an amazonomachy on display in the Painted Stoa, as follows:

> Woman is a very horsey creature; she sits tight and will not slip off when the horse runs; just look at the Amazons whom Mikon painted fighting on horseback with the men.

Such paintings were apparently judged critically for the attention paid to anatomical detail: according to Pollux (2.69), a 5th-century expert on horsemanship by the name of Simon reproached Mikon because he incorrectly painted horses with eyelashes on their lower lids. Pausanias (1.3.4) describes a painting of the Battle of Mantineia (362 B.C.) which he saw in the Stoa of Zeus Eleutherios:

19. Neck of an amphora with grazing horse, ca. 725–700 B.C. (P 22439)

20. Oinochoe with grazing horses, ca. 700 B.C. (P 24032)

21. *Horses on a Protoattic oinochoe, ca. 675–650 B.C. (P 12178, watercolor) (P. de Jong)*

22. *Amphora with two horse protomes, ca. 650–625 B.C. (P 22551)*

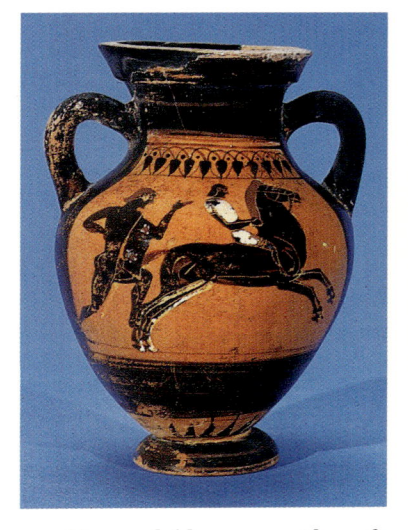

23. Horse and rider on an amphora of
ca. 540 B.C. (P 13036)

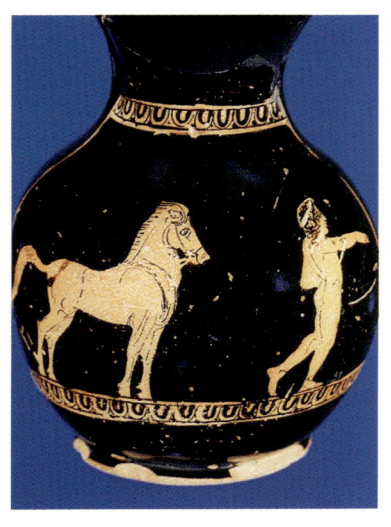

24. Red-figured chous,
late 5th century B.C. (P 23850)

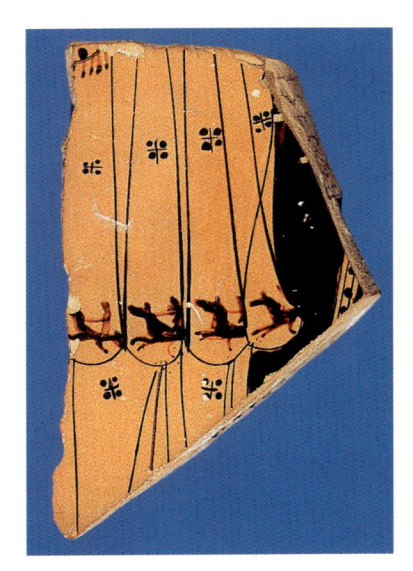

25. Red-figured sherd showing drapery
decorated with running horses and
their riders. 5th century B.C. (P 9757)

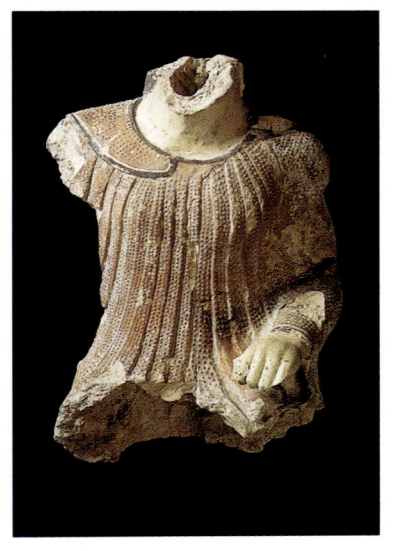

26. Torso of a terracotta rider, perhaps
from the roof of the Royal Stoa.
Late 6th century B.C. (T 4025)

27. *Two centaurs attacking Kaineus. West frieze of the Hephaisteion, ca. 450–425 B.C.*

28. *Horseman on the frieze of the Parthenon, 438–432 B.C. (A. Frantz)*

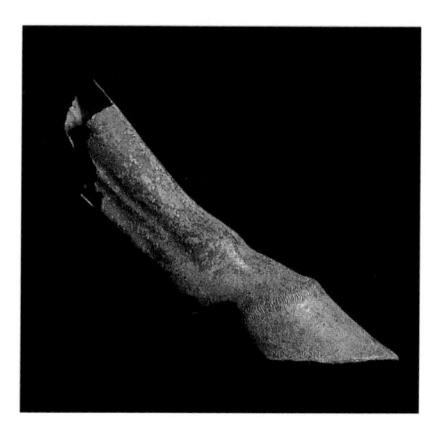

29. *Fragment of a bronze statue of a horse. The hoof, fetlock, and lower part of the leg are preserved; length ca. 0.50 m. (B 233)*

In the picture is a cavalry battle, in which the most notable figures are, among the Athenians, Grylos, the son of Xenophon, and in the Boeotian cavalry, Epaminondas the Theban. These pictures were painted for the Athenians by Euphranor.

Many Athenian buildings were also decorated with sculptures of horses. A terracotta figure of a mounted rider, about one-third lifesize and brightly painted, may well have originally adorned the roof of the Royal Stoa in the years before the Persian destruction of Athens in 480 B.C. (26). The Hephaisteion, built just above the Agora in the mid 5th century B.C., was decorated with friezes, at least one of which shows centaurs in battle (27). And the great Panathenaic frieze of the Parthenon consists largely of dozens of Athenian horsemen riding along in procession (28, 39).

Finally, there were numerous freestanding sculptures both on the Acropolis and in the Agora which depicted horses (29). Occasionally they were of the horse alone: the horse expert Simon (see above) set up a bronze statue of a horse near the Eleusinion, and one 5th-century sculptor at least, by the name of Strongylion, made his reputation in the 5th century as "an artist responsible for excellent images of cattle and horses," according to Pausanias (9.30.1). A poem of the 2nd century A.C. praises a bronze horse done by Lysippos, favorite sculptor of Alexander the Great:

30. *Gilded sword and gilded bronze leg and drapery from an equestrian statue, ca. 300 B.C. (B 1382, 1384)*

31. *A possible restoration of the statue represented in 30 in its setting on a gate at the west end of the Painted Stoa. (W. B. Dinsmoor Jr.)*

Look how proudly the art of the worker in bronze makes his horse stand. Fierce is his glance as he arches his neck and shakes out his wind-tossed mane for the course. I believe that if a charioteer were to fit the bit to his jaws and prick him with the goad, thy work, Lysippos, would surprise us by running away; for Art makes it breathe. (*Greek Anthology* 9.777)

Most commonly, horses were represented drawing chariots or with a rider. Several statues in bronze of successful generals or statesmen on horseback are known to have been set up in the Agora. The decree announcing the honor usually specified whether the figure was to be mounted. The Thracian king Audoleon (*IG* II² 654) in 285/4 B.C. and the Macedonian Asandros (*IG* II² 450) in 314/13 B.C. are two individuals known to have been so honored. The Macedonian king Demetrios Poliorcetes, who ruled Athens after the death of Alexander the Great, was also awarded an equestrian statue in the Agora. Fragments of a gilded bronze statue of a figure on horseback were found in a well, where they had been deliberately discarded in the years around 200 B.C. A sword, pieces of drapery, and the left leg are all that survive (30, 31). As all the statues of Demetrios Poliorcetes were torn down by the Athenians in 200 B.C., we may have here the remnants of the honorary statue of him set up in the Agora about a century earlier.

In all periods from the 8th century B.C. until late Roman times, small, cheap terracotta figurines of horses were available for sale in and around the Agora (32–36). Used as votive offerings to the gods and as toys, they show a wide range of skill and craftsmanship, often accurately reflecting the degree of expertise to be found in the larger works of art of their time.

HORSERACING

The aristocracy bred and raced horses (37, 38), apparently from very early times. In Book 23 of the *Iliad*—our earliest literary description of the use of the horse for sport—there is a lively and exciting account of the chariot race held as part of the funeral games of Patroklos. Homer

32, 33. Terracotta figurines of horses, 7th century B.C. (T 224, T 204)

34. Head from a terracotta figurine of a horse, 5th/4th century B.C. (T 4373)

35. Head and neck of a terracotta horse figurine, A.D. 250–300 (T 1941)

36. Terracotta horse figurine with wheels, 4th century A.C. (T 1364)

devotes more than 350 lines to this race between five heroes, won by Diomedes (*Iliad* 23.287–650). Sophokles, in his *Elektra* (lines 680–763), also includes the description of a chariot race in heroic times, one which ends in a disastrous and spectacular crash. Finally, one of the foundation myths of the Olympic games concerns a chariot race, which was later depicted in sculpture on the pediment of the Temple of Zeus at Olympia. According to the legend, King Oinomaos had a daughter, Hippodameia (tamer of horses!), whose hand he offered in marriage to any suitor who could beat him in a chariot race. If the suitor lost he was put to death, and several lost their lives until Pelops (eponymous hero of the Peloponnesos) beat Oinomaos by sabotaging his chariot. All these early accounts seem to suggest that chariot racing was the preferred form of competition, despite or perhaps because of the extraordinary danger (37, 38, 9, 10, 11).

Both horseracing and chariot races were prominent features of all four of the Panhellenic games: Olympic, Pythian (Delphi), Isthmian, and Nemean. Equestrian events were introduced at Olympia in 680 B.C., and by 400 B.C. the Olympic program included a horse race, a four-horse chariot race, and a two-horse chariot race. Other equestrian events—such as a mule-cart race and a race for mares—were tried for a while and then abandoned. No remains of a hippodrome survive at any of the four sites; this needed to be little more than a large, flat area, without much architectural embellishment, though Pausanias describes an elaborate starting device in the hippodrome at Olympia. As with stadia, the actual length of the race may have varied somewhat from site to site. The usual length of a hippodrome was two stades (about 300–400 meters). At Olympia, the four-horse chariot race (*tethrippon*) consisted of twelve laps of the course, the two-horse chariot race (*synoris*) eight laps, and the horse race (*keles*) six laps. Chariot racing was one of the most enduring aspects of pagan life in the Christian world. It was taken up with enthusiasm at Rome

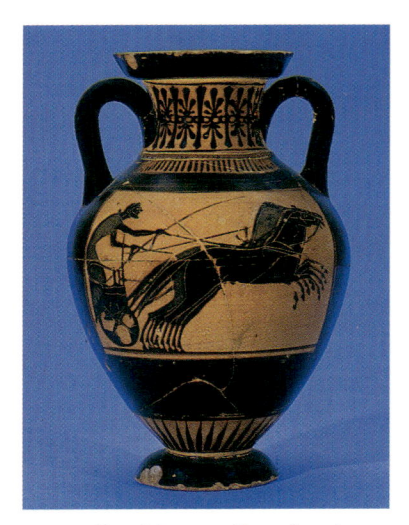

37. Quadriga *on a Panathenaic amphora, late 6th century* B.C. *(P 24661)*

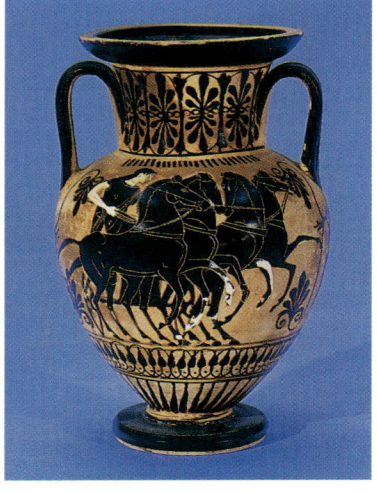

38. *Black-figured amphora with quadriga, 6th century* B.C. *(P 23200)*

and became a favored event in Constantinople, where the hippodrome was built adjoining the Imperial Palace, and racing flourished until well into the 6th century A.C.

The Athenians were regular competitors at all the Panhellenic games. In the 6th century B.C. the statesman Kimon won three four-horse chariot races at Olympia and had his horses (mares, in a sport where stallions were usually favored) buried near his own grave (Herodotos 6.103). Pindar, the great Theban poet, was hired to write an ode celebrating the victory of Megakles, son of Megakles, of Athens for his victory in the four-horse chariot race in 490 B.C. at Delphi (*Pythian 7*). And in 416 B.C., in an unprecedented display of private wealth, Alcibiades entered seven four-horse chariots in the games at Olympia, taking first, second, and fourth place. The prestige accorded both the individual and the state for such a display is expressed in Thucydides' version (6.16) of a speech given by Alcibiades to the Athenians a year or so later:

> For the Hellenes, who had previously hoped that our state had been exhausted by the war, conceived an idea of its greatness that even transcended its actual power by reason of the magnificence of my display as sacred representative at Olympia, because I entered seven chariots, a number that no private citizen had ever entered before, and won the first prize, and the second, and the fourth, and provided everything else in a style worthy of my victory. For by general custom such things do mean honor, and from what is done men also infer power. And again, although whatever display I made in the city, by providing choruses or in any other way, naturally causes jealousy among my townsmen, yet in the eyes of strangers this too gives an impression of strength. And this is no useless folly, when a man by his private expenditures benefits not himself only but also his state.

Alcibiades' assessment of the prestige such a success brought the sponsoring state is echoed in the treatment of the victors. The prize for victory in any event at these Panhellenic games was a simple crown: olive at Olympia, laurel at Delphi, pine at Isthmia, and celery at Nemea.

The honor such victories carried, however, ensured that the individuals were rewarded in other ways, both at home and at the Panhellenic sites. Pausanias records dozens of statues of victors in the games at Olympia, and from Delphi we have the magnificent bronze statue of the charioteer. The 6th-century lawgiver Solon decreed that Athenians who won at Isthmia should receive 100 drachmas, while those who won at Olympia should receive 500 (Plutarch, *Solon* 23). Athenian victors in the Panhellenic games were also invited to dine at public expense in the town hall (*prytaneion*) for the rest of their lives.

The PANATHENAIA

Special games, sacred to Athena, were part of the great Athenian festival, the Panathenaia, founded around 566 B.C. Here, too, the equestrian events were an important feature of the program, and more than a dozen are known. In addition to the usual horse and chariot races familiar from the Panhellenic games, there were numerous additional and unusual equestrian contests: races for war horses, javelin-throwing from horseback, a mounted torch race, and a mock cavalry battle (*anthippasia*). The games for the Panathenaia are unusual in that they had a panhellenic character, with events in which numerous foreigners competed, while there was also a local aspect, with events in which only Athenians could participate. Many of these latter contests were for teams assembled from the ten tribes of Athens. They seem to stress the democratic nature of Athenian society, emphasizing corporate rather than purely individual achievement, with the tribal organization reflecting the basis of the Kleisthenic democracy. Many of the events had a distinctly military aspect and, as noted, a large number were equestrian in nature. The aristocratic tendencies of the cavalry were presumably partially mitigated by the team competitions in at least some of the equestrian contests.

Unlike the crown, which was the only prize in the Panhellenic games, prizes of value were offered in the Panathenaia. Victorious tribes won oxen to be sacrificed and eaten in a great feast. Individual victors were awarded olive oil stored in special black-figured amphoras decorated

39. *Horsemen on the Parthenon frieze, possibly riding in the Panathenaic procession on the Panathenaic Way, 438–432 B.C. (A. Frantz)*

with a picture of the actual event for which the oil was a prize. It is a measure of the significance of the equestrian contests that the prize for victory in the chariot race was 140 amphoras of oil (ca. 5,600 liters), worth some 2,520 drachmas. With one drachma being roughly a laborer's daily wage, the prize was of substantial value.

The Agora was the focus for much of the Panathenaia and the associated games. In very early times most if not all of the games were probably held there, and even when a stadium, hippodrome, and theater were built elsewhere to accommodate aspects of the festival, the Agora continued as the venue for several important events. A focal point was the processional road itself, the Panathenaic Way, which ran through the Agora, leading from the main city gate (*dipylon*) at the northwest up to the Acropolis to the southeast. Along this route marched the great Panathenaic procession which, if we may judge from the depiction on the Parthenon frieze, was made up in large part

40. Base for a monument commemorating a victory in the apobates, *showing the chariot and armed warrior, 4th century* B.C. *(S 399)*

of Athenian cavalrymen (39, 28). The young horsemen of Athens, shown mounting up and riding out, must have been a prominent feature of the spectacle.

One very old-fashioned equestrian event continued to be held on the Panathenaic Way in all periods. This was the *apobates*, a chariot race in which the contestant wore armor and periodically leapt off a moving chariot and ran alongside it before leaping back on again. According to Plutarch, it was one of the most demanding of all events. It is depicted on the frieze of the Parthenon, and several monuments set up by victors have been found, one of them in the Agora (40). This event and all other uses of chariots in the games were anachronistic. They presumably hark back to much earlier times, when men fought and perhaps hunted with chariots; by the historical period chariotry played no part in Greek warfare and chariots were used only for racing and largely ceremonial occasions.

41. Fragment of a sculpted monument commemorating a tribal victory in the anthippasia, *ca. 400 B.C. (17167)*

Another major equestrian event at the Panathenaia was a mock cavalry battle, the *anthippasia*; the pageantry is described by Xenophon (*The Cavalry Commander* 3.11–12):

> In the *anthippasia* when the regiments pursue and fly from one another at the gallop in two squadrons of five regiments, each side led by its commander (*hipparch*), the regiments should ride through one another. How formidable they will look when they charge front to front, how imposing when, after sweeping across

the hippodrome, they stand facing one another again; how splendid, when the trumpet sounds and they charge once more at a quicker pace! After the halt, the trumpet should sound once more, and they should charge yet a third time at top speed; and when they have crossed, they should all range themselves in battle line preparatory to being dismissed, and ride up to the council, just as you are accustomed to do.

As noted earlier, the teams competed in tribal contingents. Though the contest took place in the hippodrome—a large level area near the sea at Phaleron, southwest of Athens—sculpted victory monuments were often set up by the winning tribe in the Agora, near its northwest corner. One such monument (41, 42), found in 1970 at the northeast corner of the Royal Stoa and dating to around 400 B.C., shows in relief a serried rank of youthful riders, followed by their older, bearded officer. Five figures are preserved and there must originally have been some fifteen to twenty riders. The officer at the rear reminds us of Xenophon's advice concerning the placement of experienced men:

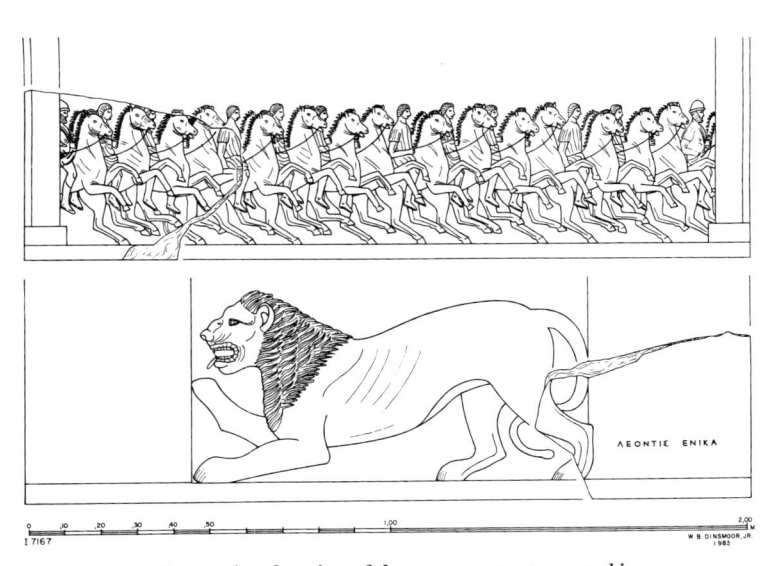

42. Restoration drawing of the monument represented in 41, showing both sides of the relief. (W. B. Dinsmoor Jr.)

43. Base for a monument commemorating a victory in the anthippasia. *A mounted horseman is approaching a victory tripod, while another side carries the inscription listing the event, the names of the winning officers, and the signature of the artist, Bryaxis. Second quarter of the 4th century B.C. (Nat. Mus. no. 1733)*

You must be very careful to appoint a competent man as leader in the rear. For if he is a good man, his cheers will always hearten the ranks in front of him in case it becomes necessary to charge; or, should the moment come to retreat, his prudent leadership will in all probability do much for the safety of his regiment. (*The Cavalry Commander* 2.5)

Preserved on the back of the piece is a rear paw and part of the tail of a lion, a punning reference to the victorious tribe Leontis (λέων = lion), as we learn from the adjacent inscription: "Leontis won the victory" (Λεοντὶς ενίκα).

A second monument celebrating a victory in the *anthippasia* was found in 1892 just behind the Royal Stoa during construction of the Athens–Peiraieus railroad (43). It is a square base of marble designed to carry a bronze tripod, a common symbol of victory. On three sides it is decorated with a relief of a mounted rider approaching a tripod. On the fourth side is an inscription of the 4th century B.C. which lists the event and the names of three victorious *phylarchs* from the tribe Pandionis. Below is the signature of the artist Bryaxis, one of the four sculptors of the Mausoleion of Halikarnassos, one of the seven wonders of the ancient world.

The ATHENIAN CAVALRY

In addition to racing events as part of the games, the other principal use of the horse in antiquity was for warfare. As in other Greek and later armies, the Athenian cavalry was an elite corps within the army. For most of its history, it was quite aristocratic in composition and represented only a tiny fraction of the fighting forces of the city. Drawn from the upper classes, the *hippeis* were often under suspicion in democratic Athens, especially late in the 5th century when, with support from the knights, the city fell under oligarchic control. The cavalry at full strength in the 5th century numbered one thousand troops, whereas the infantry would have been ten or twenty times that number and the fleet—with two hundred crew members per ship—required tens of thousands of men. In the troubled times of the early 3rd century B.C., the number of cavalrymen seems to have dropped to as low as two hundred before recovering to around five hundred.

We have a number of Athenian treatises and other written sources on the cavalry and horsemanship in antiquity. One, by Simon and dating to the 5th century B.C., survives in part. Two works written by the general and historian Xenophon in the 4th century B.C. are fully preserved: *On Horsemanship* (*Peri Hippikon*) and *The Cavalry Commander* (*Hipparchikos*). Other information concerning the cavalry comes from Aristotle, the orators, and the comic poets. Many inscriptions found in the Agora are sources of further insight. The cavalry was under the command of two senior officers, the *hipparchs*, who were seconded by ten commanders known as *phylarchs*, one chosen from each tribe. Numerous honorary inscriptions survive, rendering thanks to these officers for the conscientious performance of their duties or for the generous provision of food and equipment. These decrees, honoring individual officers or the whole staff, were passed by the state, by a single tribe, by the cavalry corps itself, and even in one instance by foreign mercenaries serving with the Athenian cavalry (44).

Other monuments were set up to honor individual commanders. The base of one such dedication was found in 1990, some twenty-five meters north of the Panathenaic Way (45). On two sides it shows horse-

44. Inscription of 281/80 B.C. honoring the cavalry officers—the hipparchs and phylarchs—of the previous year, passed by a contingent of foreign mercenary light-armed cavalry troops known as Tarantinoi. *(I 7587)*

45. Sculpted base honoring the cavalry officer Hierophanes, son of Polyaratos of Alopeke. 4th century B.C. *(I 7515)*

46. Drawing of the northwest corner of the Agora, where the Panathenaic Way enters the square, showing the Royal (left) and Painted (right) Stoas and the Crossroads Enclosure with its well (foreground). The area was known in antiquity as "The Herms." (W. B. Dinsmoor Jr.)

men with helmet and sword astride rearing horses. Above the better-preserved side is an inscription referring to the tribe, Antiochis, and the name of a man (Hierophanes, son of Polyaratos of Alopeke), presumably the officer depicted, either a *hipparch* or a *phylarch*.

The cavalry is closely associated with the Agora square, in particular the area around the northwest corner, where the main street of the city, the Panathenaic Way, entered the square between the Royal (*basileios*) and Painted (*poikile*) Stoas (46). This area was known in antiquity as "The Herms" (*Hermai*) according to Harpokration, quoting an earlier source: "From the *Poikile* and the *Basileios* stoas extend the so-called Herms." A herm was a stylized, primitive image of the god Hermes mounted on a square shaft which was decorated with a sculpted representation of the male genitalia. Herms were used to mark crossroads, doors, and entrances, and dozens of examples set up at the northwest entrance to the Agora have been found in the excavations. The association of the cavalry with the Herms is indicated by a fragment written by the comic poet Mnesimachos in the 4th century B.C.:

47. The Crossroads Enclosure from the north, showing the stone well-head just in front of it. Various pieces of archival material concerning the cavalry were found in this well, which was in use from the 5th into the 2nd century B.C.

48. Clay tokens stamped with the name of Pheidon, the hipparch on Lemnos, from the Crossroads Well. 4th century B.C.

Go forth from the chambers roofed with cypress wood, Manes; go to the Agora, to the Herms, the place frequented by the *phylarchs*, and to their handsome pupils, whom Pheidon trains in mounting and dismounting. (quoted in Athenaeus 9.402 ff.)

Excavation of a well (46, 47) at the northwest corner of the Agora has produced an extraordinary correlation of literary and archaeological evidence. Twenty-six round clay tokens were found, stamped with the name Pheidon of Thria, the *hipparch* on Lemnos (48). Lemnos was an Athenian island possession staffed with Athenian military officers, and it seems certain that the comic fragment and the clay tokens found in the area of the Herms refer to the same individual. Xenophon also envisions the cavalry performing in the Agora, near the Herms:

As for the processions, I think they would be most pleasing to both the gods and the spectators if they included a gala ride in the Agora. The starting point would be the Herms; and the cavalry would ride around saluting the gods at their shrines and statues. . . . When the circuit is completed and the cavalcade is again near the Herms, the next thing to do, I think, is to gallop at top speed by tribes to the Eleusinion. (*The Cavalry Commander* 3.2)

In all probability, the cavalry trained on the wide, packed gravel surface of the Panathenaic Way itself where it ran through the Agora; the situation is reminiscent of Elis, where the agora was known as the hippodrome because the citizens trained and exercised their horses there. At several points along the Panathenaic Way stone troughs or basins appropriate for watering horses have been found (49), and an iron ring set into a marble block beside the roadway may have served as a hitching post (50). Regular training would have been necessary as the ancient Greek horseman, to judge from thousands of representations, had the benefit of neither saddle nor—more important—stirrups; maintaining one's seat, particularly while wielding a weapon, must have taken great skill.

Two buildings closely associated with the cavalry also probably stood near the northwest corner of the Agora square. One was the *hipparcheion*, office of the cavalry commanders, and the other was the Stoa of the

49. Limestone basin found near the Panathenaic Way at the southeast corner of the Agora, perhaps used as a watering trough; length ca. 1.0 m. 5th/4th century B.C. (A 3649)

50. Marble block with attached iron ring, perhaps used as a hitching post. Found along the edge of the Panathenaic Way (in background, bordered by stone gutter), east of the Temple of Ares. View looking east.

51. Drawings of two lead tablets from the cavalry archive found in the Crossroads Well. a. "Of Konon, a chestnut with a centaur [brand], value 700 drachmas." b. "Of Dexandros of Anaph[lystos], a chestnut, unbranded, value 700 drachmas." 3rd century B.C. (IL 1563, 1551) (H. Besi)

Herms. Neither building has been recognized or uncovered as yet, but archival material relating to the cavalry which was stored or displayed in these two buildings has been found clustered in the northwest area.

An archive of the cavalry dating to the 4th and 3rd centuries B.C. was found in the same well which produced the Pheidon tokens. It consists of several dozen inscribed thin lead strips (51). Measuring about 0.02 by 0.10 m, each was inscribed with a man's name, the color of his horse, a description of its brand (a symbol such as a centaur, ax, trident, or snake), and a price falling somewhere between 500 and 1,200 drachmas, the average being about 700 drachmas (two years' wages). Analysis of these tablets suggests that they are the record of the annual evaluation (τίμησις) of the cavalry. The information preserved on them would allow the state to properly compensate a cavalryman if his horse was lost in battle. The tablets became obsolete at the end of each year; normally they were erased and reused, but in several instances they were thrown into two wells, one in the Agora and another by the Dipylon Gate.

The same Agora Crossroads Well (47) also produced nine small round lead disks (0.02 m in diameter), each stamped with the representation of a piece of armor (helmet, corselet, shield, greaves) on one side and with a letter on the other (52). Written sources are silent as to their use, but it seems likely that they were tokens to be exchanged for

52. Lead tokens depicting pieces of armor (helmet, breastplate, shield, greaves) probably distributed to members of the cavalry. Found in the Crossroads Well, 3rd century B.C. (IL 1572–1579)

actual pieces of equipment distributed to the cavalrymen from the state arsenal.

The Pheidon tokens, lead strips, and armor tokens all come from the same well and suggest the nearby location of the *hipparcheion*; several inscribed stelai, honoring various cavalry officers and found in the immediate vicinity, were set up in the Stoa of the Herms. Together with the sculpted monuments celebrating victory in the equestrian games, they suggest that the northwest corner of the square was the focal point of activity for the Athenian cavalry within the city.

OTHER EQUIDS

Both the donkey and the mule were certainly known and used in antiquity (53–55). Mules were employed both for riding and for drawing carts; from 500 B.C. on there were actually mule-cart races in the Olympic games, and one of Pindar's odes celebrates such a victory (*Olympian* 6, 468 B.C.). Yet what must have been a somewhat undignified event did not maintain its popularity, and it was abandoned in 444 B.C.

53. Mule on a fragment of a large closed vessel, ca. 650 B.C. (P 22691)

54. Herakles on a mule. Terracotta plaque of the early 1st century B.C. (T 2466)

55. Satyr on a donkey. Red-figured cup by Epiktetos, ca. 500 B.C. (P 24114)

One old Athenian mule, who worked long and hard on the construction of the Parthenon, is said by Aelian to have been fed at public expense in the town hall (*prytaneion*) for the remainder of its life. Donkeys, as today, were used primarily for riding and as beasts of burden. Often associated with the god Dionysos and his rowdy, drunken followers, they are readily identified on painted pots by their characteristic long ears and evidence of sexual arousal. Remains of a donkey were found in the kitchen of a house, a victim of the destruction of Athens by the Herulians in A.D. 267 (56).

Ancient Athenian literature is full of references to the horse, which played a significant role in Athenian social, political, and military life. Athenian sculptors, painters, and potters found horses a popular subject from the beginnings of Greek art to the end of antiquity. The excavation of cavalry archives and victory monuments, as well as the roadway used for processions and the training of horses, has shown that the Agora, focus of so much of Athenian life, was also for centuries the center of equestrian activity in the ancient city.

56. Skeletal remains of a donkey as found in the kitchen of a house destroyed by the Herulians in A.D. 267.